Is The New Testament Reliable?

By Phil Fernandes

Is the New Testament Reliable?
by Dr. Phil Fernandes

Printed in the United States of America

ISBN-13: 978-1723496318
ISBN-10: 1723496316

IBD Press
P. O. Box 3264
Bremerton, WA 98310
www.philfernandes.com

Dedication

This book is dedicated to:

my wife Cathy

and

my former professor and mentor Dr. Norman Geisler

About the Author

Dr. Phil Fernandes is the senior pastor of Trinity Bible Fellowship and the president of the Institute of Biblical Defense. Fernandes teaches apologetics, philosophy, and ethics at Crosspoint Academy, Veritas International University, Columbia Evangelical Seminary, and Shepherds Bible College. He has earned a Ph.D. in philosophy of religion from Greenwich University, a Doctor of Theological Studies from Columbia Evangelical Seminary, and a Master of Arts in Religion from Liberty University. Fernandes is completing work on a Doctor of Ministry in Apologetics Degree through Southern Evangelical Seminary. He is a member of the following professional societies: The Evangelical Theological Society, the Society of Christian Philosophers, the Evangelical Philosophical Society, and the International Society of Christian Apologetics. Dr. Fernandes has publicly debated some of America's leading atheists at schools such as Princeton University and the University of North Carolina at Chapel Hill. He has authored several books dealing with the defense of the Christian faith. Hundreds of Dr. Fernandes' lectures, debates, and sermons can be downloaded from his websites:

www.philfernandes.com

and

www.instituteofbiblicaldefense.com.

Other Books Authored or Co-Authored by Phil Fernandes:

The God Who Sits Enthroned: Evidence for God's Existence
(Xulon Press, 2002)

No Other Gods: A Defense of Biblical Christianity
(Xulon Press, 2002)

God, Government, and the Road to Tyranny:
A Christian View of Government and Morality
(Xulon Press, 2003; co-authored with Eric Purcell, Kurt Rinear, and
Rorri Wiesinger)

Decay of a Nation: The Need for National Revival
(Triune Press, 1987; no longer in print)

Theism versus Atheism: The Internet Debate
(IBD Press, 1997, 2000; co-authored with Dr. Michael Martin)

Contend Earnestly for the Faith: A Survey of Christian Apologetics
(Publish America, 2007)

The Atheist Delusion: A Christian Response to Christopher Hitchens
and Richard Dawkins
(Xulon Press, 2009)

Evidence for Faith: Essays in Christian Apologetics
(IBD Press, 2009: co-authored with Gary Tronson and Erik Stenerson)

Seven Great Apologists: Seven Defenders of the Faith Who Impacted
Their World
(IBD Press, 2011)

Hijacking the Historical Jesus: Answering Recent Attacks on the Jesus of the Bible
(IBD Press, 2012; co-authored with Kyle Larson)

Is Hell Forever? Does the Bible Teach That Hell will be Annihilation or Eternal Torment?
(co-authored with Chris Date)

The Fernandes Guide to Apologetic Methodologies
(IBD Press, 2016)

Vital Issues in the Inerrancy Debate
(Wipf and Stock, 2015; co-authored with David Farnell, Norman Geisler, Joe Holden, and Bill Roach)

Dr. Fernandes also contributed to the following books:

The Big Argument: Does God Exist? Twenty-Four Scholars Explore How Science, Archaeology, and Philosophy Haven't Disproved God
(Master Books, 2006; edited by John Ashton and Michael Westacott)

Harvest Handbook on Christian Apologetics
(Harvest House Publishers, 2018; edited by Joseph Holden)

Chapter One
Are Miracles Possible?

Atheists believe that belief in miracles is pre-scientific superstition, and that no rational person would accept the possibility of a miracle actually occurring. They act as if before Charles Darwin came along mankind didn't know that a virgin birth or a bodily resurrection could not be explained through natural laws. Even the ancients understood that virgins do not normally give birth to babies and that dead people stay dead. That's why the ancients believed the virgin birth and bodily resurrection of Jesus were miracles—because the laws of nature were superseded. The new atheists are biased against the possibility of miracles. They begin their assessment of Christianity by assuming (without proof) that miracles are impossible, and then reject the Gospel accounts because of its miracle claims.

Christianity is a religion based in history. The claims, death, and resurrection of Jesus of Nazareth occurred in history. For this reason, historical evidence is of great importance. If one can prove that Jesus really did rise from the dead in history, then one will have gone a long way towards establishing Christianity as the true religion. However, before an apologist can engage in presenting historical evidences for the resurrection of Christ, he must first answer the philosophical objections against the possibility of miracles. If miracles are by definition impossible, then it makes no sense to look into history to see if Jesus really rose from the dead.

The strongest philosophical argumentation against miracles came from the pens of Benedict Spinoza (1632-1677) and David Hume (1711-1776). Spinoza was a pantheist.[1] He believed in an impersonal god that was identical to the universe. He reasoned that an impersonal god could not choose to perform miracles, for only personal beings make choices. Whatever an impersonal god does, it must do by necessity. Spinoza believed that nature necessarily operates in a uniform manner. Therefore, he argued that the laws of nature cannot be violated. Since miracles would be violations of the laws of nature, they are impossible.[2]

David Hume was a deist. He believed that after God created the universe, He no longer involved Himself with His creation. Hume reasoned that miracles, if they occur, are very rare events. On the other hand, the laws of nature describe repeatable, everyday occurrences. Hume argued that the wise man will always base his beliefs on the highest degree of probability. Since the laws of nature have a high degree of probability while a miracle is improbable, Hume considered the evidence against miracles always greater than the evidence for miracles. Therefore, according to Hume, the wise man will always reject the proposed miracle.[3]

---

[1]Norman L. Geisler, *Miracles and the Modern Mind* (Grand Rapids: Baker Book House, 1992), 18
[2]Ibid., 15.

[3]David Hume, *An Inquiry Concerning Human Understanding* (New York: The Liberal Arts press, 1955), 117-141.

Response to Spinoza

Spinoza argued that miracles are impossible. Several things should be mentioned in refutation of Spinoza's argument. Though it is true that a pantheistic god cannot choose to perform a miracle (a pantheistic god is impersonal and, therefore, cannot choose anything), there is strong evidence that a pantheistic god does not exist.[4] As the cosmological argument has shown, a theistic God exists.[5] A theistic God is a personal God, and a personal God *can* choose to perform miracles.

Second, Spinoza's premise that the laws of nature can never be violated is suspect. The laws of nature are descriptive; they are not prescriptive. In other words, the laws of nature describe the way nature usually acts. The laws of nature do not prescribe how nature must act.[6]

Third, Spinoza's definition of a miracle as a violation of the laws of nature is objectionable. It is possible that miracles do not violate the laws of nature; they merely supersede the laws of nature. C. S. Lewis argued along these lines.[7]

Fourth, if God created the universe, then the laws of nature are subject to Him. God can choose to suspend or violate (depending on how one defines a miracle) the laws of nature any time He wishes. In short, Spinoza has failed to show that miracles are impossible.

---

[4]A pantheistic God cannot explain the existence of evil, absolute moral laws, personality, the beginning of the universe, meaning in life, etc.

[5]See Norman L. Geisler, *Christian Apologetics* (Grand Rapids: baker Book House, 1976), 237-259.

[6]Terry L. Miethe, ed. *Did Jesus Rise from the Dead?* (San Francisco: Harper and Row, 1987), 18.

[7]C. S. Lewis, *Miracles* (New York: Collier Books, 1960), 59-60.

Response to Hume

Hume, unlike Spinoza, did not argue for the impossibility of miracles. Instead, he argued that miracles were so unlikely that the evidence against them will always be greater than the evidence for them. Hume argued that miracles are improbable, and that the wise man will only believe that which is probable. Hence, the wise man will never accept evidence for a miracle.[8]

The Christian apologist can respond to Hume's reasoning in the following manner. Just because usual events (the laws of nature) occur more often does not mean that the wise man will never believe that an unusual event (a miracle) has occurred.[9] The wise man should not *a priori* rule out the possibility of miracles. The wise man will examine the evidence for or against a miracle claim, and base his judgment on the evidence. Since there were over 500 witnesses who claimed to have seen Jesus risen from the dead (1 Corinthians 15:3-8), a wise man would not reject the miracle of the resurrection merely because all other men have remained dead. It seems that a wise man would examine a miracle claim if there are reliable eyewitnesses. If there is no good reason to reject the testimony of reliable eyewitnesses, it seems that a wise man would accept their testimony that a miracle has occurred.

Contemporary Western Academic Bias Against Miracles

Contemporary anthropological studies have shown that the non-Western world does not agree with the Western academic bias against miracles. In fact, many current anthropologists accuse Western scholars who are biased against miracles of ethnocentrism—believing their culture is superior to other cultures.[10]

---

[8]Geisler, *Miracles*, 23-28.
[9]Ibid., 27-31.

Also, even Westerners in general do not agree with the Western academic bias against miracles. Recent surveys show that over 80% of Americans still believe that miracles are possible.[11] So, outside of the Western academic establishment, most people are willing to examine evidence for or against miracles—they are open to the possibility of miracles. It appears that Western scholars who have a bias against miracles are not only out of touch with the non-Western world, but they are apparently out of touch with most Westerners as well. The Western academic bias against miracles is not justified. Miracle claims should be investigated, rather than ruled out in a biased, a priori manner.

Some people will not accept any event unless it has a natural cause. Therefore, they reject miracles because they have a supernatural Cause (God).[12] But, the cosmological argument has shown that the universe itself needs a supernatural Cause (God). Therefore, if there is a God who created the universe, then He would have no problem intervening in His universe by supernaturally working miracles within it. A person cannot rule out miracles simply because his world view does not allow them. If his world view is weak (such as pantheism and deism), then he has weak reasons for rejecting miracles. If, on the other hand, a person has strong evidence for his world view (such as theism), and that world view is consistent with the reality of miracles, then that person has strong reasons for believing that miracles are possible.

This chapter has only shown that miracles are possible. Historical evidence must be examined to see whether miracles have actually occurred. Philosophical argumentation can only show that miracles are possible. Historical evidences must be utilized to determine if an alleged miracle (such as the resurrection of Jesus from the dead) has in fact occurred.

---

[10] Gregory Boyd and Paul Eddy, *The Jesus Legend* (Grand Rapids: Baker Book House, 2007), 67-90.

[11] Ibid.

[12] Ibid., 50-51.

Chapter Two
The Historical Reliability of the New Testament

Christianity is a religion with deep historical roots. For example, if Jesus did not rise from the dead (a historical event), then the Christian Faith cannot save (1 Cor. 15:14, 17). If He did not die on the cross for the sins of mankind (a historical event), then Christianity offers no hope (1 Pet. 2:24; 3:18). Proving the New Testament can be trusted will go a long way to establishing Christianity as the one true faith.

This booklet will attempt to show that if we use honest, neutral presuppositions in our study of the New Testament, we will see that it is historically reliable. It can be shown that the New Testament accounts were written by eyewitnesses who knew Christ, or persons who knew the eyewitnesses. This booklet will not deal with defending the Bible as the inspired and inerrant Word of God; the purpose of this chapter is to merely show that the New Testament documents can be shown to be historically reliable when the researcher does not use biased, liberal presuppositions. Further argumentation is needed to establish the inspiration and inerrancy of Scripture.

6

Manuscript Evidence for the New Testament

Many historical scholars believe that one cannot know the true Jesus of history since no one no has the original writings of those who knew Him. Only copies of the originals are in existence today. Ironically, these historical scholars will often quote from Plato, as well as other ancient writers, as if they can know with certainty what Plato originally wrote. This clearly unveils a double standard: ancient secular writings can be trusted based on late copies, but the New Testament cannot be trusted since the original manuscripts are missing!

Any honest examination of the manuscript evidence will reveal that the New Testament is by far the most reliable ancient writing in existence today. There exist today nearly 24,000 hand-written copies (5,856 of them in the original Greek language) of the New Testament, either in whole or in part.[13] This should be compared with the fact that only 238 copies presently exist of Plato's Tetralogies and 36 copies of Tacitus's Annals.[14] Homer's Iliad is in second place behind the New Testament among ancient writings with about 1,900 copies.[15]

The earliest copy of Plato's Tetralogies is dated over 600 years after Plato supposedly wrote the original.[16] Compare this with the earliest extant copy of the New Testament: the John Ryland's Papyri. It contains a portion of John 18. This fragment is dated at about 130 AD or earlier, only 35 years after the original is thought to have been written.[17]

---

[13] Josh McDowell and Seam McDowell, *Evidence that Demands a Verdict.* (Nashville: Thomas Nelson Publishers, 2017), 52. See also Norman Geisler and Frank Turek, *I Don't Have Enough Faith to be an Atheist* (Wheaton: Crossway Books, 2004), 225.

[14] Ibid., 56.

[15] Ibid.

[16] Ibid.

[17] Ibid.

In fact, based on the research of a distinguished German papyrologist named Carsten P. Thiede, there are possibly even earlier New Testament fragments that were found among the Dead Sea Scrolls. One fragment is called 7Q5; it is dated earlier than 70AD. Though there is heated debate about this manuscript, it has been argued that it is a part of Mark 6:52-53.[18] Another possible New Testament fragment found in cave 7 of the Dead Sea Scrolls is 7Q4, identified by Thiede as 1 Timothy 3:16-4:3.[19] Thiede builds upon the work of the late papyrologist Jose O'Callaghan and makes a solid case that these fragments can only be identified as from Mark 6 and 1 Timothy 3 and 4. Thiede states that the only reason why New Testament scholars reject these fragments as being from the New Testament is due to their critical theories, which we have shown to be based upon biased presuppositions.[20] Carsten B. Thiede has also argued that three tiny fragments of the twenty-sixth chapter of Matthew's Gospel which belong to Magdalen College, Oxford, date to the mid first century AD.[21]

Still, even if one rejects the conclusions drawn by Thiede, we must remember there is no debate about the early dating of the John chapter eighteen fragment. So a gap of only twenty-five years is established. Again, Homer's Iliad takes second place among ancient writings, second only to the New Testament. The earliest copy of any portion of Homer's Iliad is dated about 400 years after the original writing.[22]

---

[18]Carsten P. Thiede, *Rekindling the Word* (Valley Forge: Trinity Press, 1995), 50, 114.

[19]Ibid., 174.

[20]Ibid., 169-174.

[21]Thiede, Carsten P. and Matthew D'Ancona, *Eyewitness to Jesus* (New York: Doubleday, 1996), 1-2.

[22]McDowell, *Evidence* 43.

When the contents of the extant manuscripts of the New Testament are compared, there appears to be 99.5% agreement. There is total agreement in the doctrines taught; the corruptions are mainly grammatical.[23] Homer's Iliad once again takes second place behind the New Testament among ancient documents. Homer's Iliad has a 95% accuracy when its copies are compared.[24] When one compares the accuracy of the New Testament copies with that of Homer's Iliad, one can appreciate the extreme care that went into the copying of the New Testament. For the 99.5% accuracy of the New Testament copies means that only 5 letters out of every one-thousand are in question. On the other hand, the second place 95% accuracy of the Homer's Iliad manuscripts means that 50 letters out of every one-thousand are in question. This makes the New Testament manuscripts ten times more accurate than any other ancient writng! It should also be noted that, with the high number of New Testament manuscripts and the high degree of agreement between Testament copies, we can arrive at an exact replica of the original New Testament.

The manuscript evidence for the New Testament can be clearly seen when we examine the following data adapted from a chart found in Josh and Sean McDowell's *Evidence that Demands a Verdict:*[25]

Comparison of Ancient Writings

Author	Writings	Date Written	Earliest Copies	Time Gap	No. of Copies
Homer	*Iliad*	800 BC	415 BC	400 yrs.	1,900

[23]Ibid.

[24]Ibid.
[25]Josh and Sean McDowell, *Evidence*, 52, 56.

9

Herodotus	*History*	480-425 BC	150-50 BC	330 yrs.	106
Thucydides	*History*	5th Century BC	3rd Century BC	200 yrs.	188
Plato	*Tetralogies*	400 BC	3rd Century BC	600 yrs.	238
Demosthenes	*Speeches*	4th Century BC	1st Century BC	1,400 yrs	444
Caesar	*Gallic Wars*	50s BC	9th Century AD	850 yrs.	251
Livy	*History of Rome*	59 BC-17AD	4th century AD	300 yrs.	473
Tacitus	*Annals*	AD 100	850 AD	750 yrs.	36
Pliny Secundus	*Natural History*	23-79 AD	5th Century AD	300 yrs.	200
New Testament		AD 50-100	130 AD (fragment)	30 yrs.	
			200 AD (books)	100 yrs.	Nearly 5,700 Greek copies
			250 AD Most of N.T.	150 yrs.	Nearly 24,000

				325 AD (complete N.T.)	225 yrs.		copies total

In short, historical scholars can consider the extant New Testament manuscripts to be reliable and accurate representations of what the authors originally wrote. Since the New Testament is by far the most accurately copied ancient writing, to question its authenticity is to call into question all of ancient literature.

The following manuscripts are some of the better known copies of the New Testament. The John Rylands Papyri is the oldest undisputed fragment of the New Testament still in existence. It is dated between 125 and 130 AD. It contains a portion of John 18.[26] The Bodmer Papyrus II contains most of John's Gospel and dates between 150 and 200 AD.[27] The Chester Beatty Papyri includes major portions of the New Testament; it is dated around 200 AD. Codex Vaticanus contains nearly the entire Bible and is dated between 325 and 350 AD. Codex Sinaiticus contains nearly all of the New Testament and approximately half of the Old Testament. It is dated at about 350 AD. Codex Alexandrinus encompasses almost the entire Bible and was copied around 400 AD. Codex Ephraemi represents every New Testament book except for 2 John and 2 Thessalonians. Ephraemi is dated in the 400's AD.[28]

---

[26]McDowell, *Evidence*, 46.

[27]Ibid., 46-47.
[28]Ibid., 47-48.

Ancient Greek New Testament Copies

Manuscript	Contents	Date
John Rylands Papyir	Portion of John 18	130 AD or earlier
Bodmer Papyrus II	Most of John's Gospel	150-200 AD
Chester Beatty Papyri	Major portions of the N.T.	200 AD
Codex Vaticanus	Almost entire Bible	325-350 AD
Codex Sinaiticus	All of N.T. & half of O.T.	350 AD
Codex Alexandrinus	Almost entire Bible	400 AD
Codex Ephraemi	Most of N.T.	400's AD

The very early dates of these manuscripts provide strong evidence that the content of the current New Testament is one and the same with the original writings of the apostles. There is no logical reason to doubt the reliability of these manuscripts.

It should also be noted that, besides ancient Greek manuscript copies of the New Testament, there there also exist today ancient New Testament copies in other languages. The *Old Syriac Version* and the *Syriac Peshitta* date back to the fourth and fifth centuries, yet experts believe they were copies of second century New Testament manuscripts. The *Old Latin Version* of the New Testament and the *African Old Latin Version* also show signs of having been copied from second century manuscripts.[29]

After assessing the manuscript evidence for the reliability of the New Testament, the world renown manuscript expert Sir Frederick Kenyon stated:

---

[29]McDowell, *New Evidence*, 41.

The interval then between the dates of original composition and the earliest extant evidence becomes so small as to be negligible, and the last foundation for any doubt that the Scriptures have come down to us substantially as they were written has now been removed. Both the authenticity and the general integrity of the books of the New Testament may be regarded as finally established.[30]

The Testimony of the Apostolic Fathers

The New Testament manuscript copies are not the only evidence for the reliability of the New Testament. Another source of evidence is found in the writings of the apostolic fathers. The apostolic fathers were leaders in the early church who knew the apostles and their doctrine.[31] Most of their writings were produced between 60 and 130 AD.

As we have shown, liberal scholars have attempted to find the so-called true Jesus of history. It was their goal to find a non-supernatural Jesus who never claimed to be God. These scholars believe that Christ's claim to be God and Savior, and His miraculous life (especially His bodily resurrection from the dead) are merely legends. The true Jesus of history was a great teacher; still, He was merely a man.[32] Therefore, if it can be shown that early church leaders, who personally knew the apostles, taught that the miraculous aspects of Christ's life actually occurred and that Jesus did in fact make the bold claims recorded in the New Testament, then the legend hypothesis fails. Historians recognize

---

[30]Kenyon, Frederic. *The Bible and Archeology* (New York: Harper, 1940), 288.

[31]Cairns, Earl E. *Christianity Through the Centuries*. Grand Rapids: Zondervan Publishing House, 1981), 73.

[32] Gary R. Habermas, *Ancient Evidence for the Life of Jesus* (Nashville: Thomas Nelson Publishers, 1984), 42.

that legends take generations to develop.[33] A legend is a ficticious story that, through the passage of time, many people come to accept as historically accurate. A legend can begin to develop only if the eyewitnesses and those who knew the eyewitnesses are already dead. Otherwise, the eyewitnesses or those who knew them would refute the legend. Therefore, a legend begins to compete with the historical facts a generation or two after the event or person in question has passed. However, before a legend receives wide acceptance, several generations (sometimes centuries) are needed, for there is still a remembrance of the person or event due to information passed on orally from generation to generation. After several centuries, new generations arise without the sufficient knowledge of the person or event necessary to refute the legend. If a written record compiled by eyewitnesses is passed on to future generations (as is the case with the New Testament), legends can be easily refuted.

A. N. Sherwin-White, a historian who specialized in ancient Greek and Roman history, has studied the development of ancient legends. He concluded that more than two generations are needed for legendary speculation to wipe out core historical facts.[34] When we read the apostolic fathers—those trained by the apostles themselves—we find the same teachings about the person and work of Jesus found in the New Testament. Hence, there was insufficient time for legends to develop.

One apostolic father, Clement, was the Bishop of Rome. Before he became bishop, he wrote his letter to the Corinthians in 70 AD.[35] The following is a brief quote from this letter:

---

[33] Josh McDowell and Bill Wilson, *He Walked Among Us* (San Bernardino: Here's Life Publishers, 1988), 130.

[34] Sherwin-White, A. N. Sherwin-White, *Roman Society and Roman Law in the New Testament* (Oxford: Clarendon, 1963), 188-191.

[35] John A. T. Robinson, *Redating the New Testament*. Eugene: Wipf and Stock Publishers, 1976), 327-325. Robinson argues that Clement of Rome's letter to the Corinthians had to be written, at the latest, in early 70 AD since Clement states that the temple is still standing when he wrote the letter (41.2).

Let us fear the Lord Jesus (Christ), whose blood was given for us. . .
The Apostles received the Gospel for us from the Lord Jesus Christ;
Jesus Christ was sent from God. . . He made the Lord Jesus Christ the
firstfruit, when He raised Him from the dead.[36]

It is important to note that Clement of Rome referred to Jesus as "the
Lord." This is an obvious reference to Christ's deity, for he uses the
Greek word "Kurios" with the definite article—Christ was the Lord, not
a Lord.[37] Clement also spoke of Christ's blood as being shed for us,
indicating a belief in Christ's saving work. He declared that the apostles
received the Gospel directly from Jesus. Clement also spoke of God
raising Jesus from the dead. If any of these statements were opposed to
the doctrines of the apostles, the Apostle John, who was still alive at the
time, would have openly confronted this first century bishop. However,
he did not. Therefore, the writings of Clement of Rome provide strong
confirmation of the original message of the Apostles. Contrary to the
wishful thinking of skeptics, the teachings of the first century church are
exactly what one finds in today's New Testament.

The apostolic father, Ignatius, bishop of Antioch, wrote his letters
around 107 AD. During that time, he was travelling from Antioch to
Rome to be martyred.[38] Ignatius openly wrote about the deity of Christ.
He referred to Jesus as "Jesus Christ our God," "God in man," and
"Jesus Christ the God."[39] Ignatius stated that "there is one God who

---

[36]J. B. Lightfoot and J. R. Harmer. Translators. *The Apostolic Fathers*
(Grand Rapids: Baker Book House, 1984), 67, 75. 68.

[37]Ibid., 17.

[38]Ibid., 97.

[39]Ibid., 137, 139, 149-150, 156.

manifested Himself through Jesus Christ His Son."[40] Besides ascribing deity to Christ, Ignatius also wrote of salvation in Christ and expressed belief in Christ's virgin birth, crucifixion, and resurrection. He referred to Jesus as "Christ Jesus our Savior" and wrote "Jesus Christ, who dies for us, that believing on His death ye might escape death."[41] Ignatius also wrote concerning Jesus:

> He is truly of the race of David according to the flesh, but Son of God by the Divine will and power, truly born of a virgin. . . . Be ye deaf therefore, when any man speaketh to you apart from Jesus Christ, who was born of the race of David, who was the Son of Mary, who was truly born and ate and drank, was truly persecuted under Pontius Pilate, was truly crucified and died in the sight of those in heaven and those on earth and those under the earth; who moreover was truly raised from the dead, His Father having raised Him . . .[42]

The writings of Ignatius show that only ten to fifteen years after the death of the Apostle John the central doctrines of the New Testament were already being taught. It is highly unlikely that the New Testament manuscripts, referenced by Ignatius, could have been corrupted in such a short amount of time. It is also important to remember that Clement of Rome taught the same doctrines while the Apostle John was still alive.

Another apostolic father named Polycarp (70-156 AD) was the Bishop of Smyrna. He was a personal pupil of the Apostle John.[43] Had any of the other apostolic fathers perverted the teachings of the apostles, Polycarp would have set the record straight. However, Polycarp's

---

[40]Ibid., 144.

[41]Ibid., 137, 141.

[42]Ibid., 156, 148.

[43]Cairns, 74.

16

teachings are essentially the same as that of Clement of Rome and Ignatius. Of all the apostolic fathers, Polycarp probably knew better than any the content of the original apostles' message. Liberal scholars display tremendous arrogance when they assume that they have more insight into the original apostolic message than Polycarp. Polycarp studied under the Apostle John (85-95 AD?); contemporary scholars live nearly 2,000 years later. In his letter to the Philippians, Polycarp wrote the following about 110 AD:

> . . . Jesus Christ who took our sins in His own body upon the tree, who did no sin, neither was guile found in His mouth, but for our sakes He endured all things, that we might live in Him. . . . For they loved not the present world, but Him that died for our sakes and was raised by God for us. . . . who shall believe on our Lord and God Jesus Christ and on His Father that raised Him from the dead.[44]

Here we see that Polycarp called Jesus "our Lord and God," and proclaimed Jesus' sacrificial death for us and His resurrection from the dead. If the apostles did not teach such things, then why would their successors?

While discussing the writings of Clement of Rome, Ignatius, and Polycarp, Christian scholar Paul Barnett points out that, by 110 AD, these three early church leaders quoted from or referred to twenty-five of the twenty-seven New Testament books, proving that the entire New Testament was in circulation and accepted as authoritative by the early church by the close of the first century AD. Barnett adds that "The silence of Clement, Ignatius, and Polycarp with respect to 2 John and Jude need not imply that these books were not written, only that those authors failed to quote from them or refer to them."[45]

---

[44]Lightfoot and Harmer, 180-181.

[45]Paul Barnett, *Is the New Testament Reliable?* (Downers Grove: InterVarsity Press, 2003), 40-41.

Another student of the Apostle John was Papias, the Bishop of Hierapolis. Papias was born between 60 and 70 AD and died between 130 and 140 AD. Papias wrote that he did not accept the words of any self-proclaimed teacher. Instead, he would talk to others who, like himself, had known at least one of the original apostles. In this way, Papias could discover the teachings of Christ from the sources closest to Christ Himself, rather than rely on hearsay testimony.[46]

Papias wrote of his discussions with persons who spoke with with apostles such as Andrew, Peter, Philip, Thomas, James, John, or Matthew. Papias stated that Mark received the information for his Gospel from the Apostle Peter himself. Papias also related that Matthew originally recorded his gospel in Hebrew, but that it was later translated into Greek to reach a wider audience.[47]

The testimony of the first-century and early second-century church should be considered extremely reliable. Many of these early Christians were martyred for their beliefs. Since people will only die for what they truly believe, it is reasonable to conclude that the early church sincerely believed thay were protecting the true apostolic faith from possible perversions. If they had tampered with the teachings of the apostles, they certainly would not have died for their counterfeit views.

The following conclusions can now be drawn: first, the apostolic fathers form an unbroken chain from the apostles to their day. Second, people who personally knew the apostles accepted the leadership of the apostolic fathers. Third, the apostolic fathers taught essentially the same thing as the New Testament. Fourth, the apostolic fathers and their followers were willing to die for the teachings passed down to them from the apostles themselves. Therefore, our New Testament accurately represents the teachings of the apostles. This includes such key doctrines as the deity of Christ, His substitutionary death, virgin birth, bodily resurrection, and salvation through Him alone.

------

[46]Lightfoot and Harmer, 514, 527-528.
[47]Ibid., 528-529.

The Testimony of Ancient Secular Writers

Besides references to Christ in Christian literature which date back to the first and second centuries AD, there are also ancient secular writings which refer to Christ from that same time period. The significance of these non-Christian writings is that, though the secular authors themselves did not believe the early church's message, they stated the content of what the early church actually taught.

In 52 AD, Thallus recorded a history of the Eastern Mediterranean world. In this work, he covered the time period from the Trojan War (mid 1200s BC) to his day (52 AD). Though no manuscripts of Thallus' work are known to currently exist, Julius Africanus (writing in 221 AD) referred to Thallus' work. Africanus stated that Thallus attempted to explain away the darkness that covered the land when Christ was crucified. Thallus attributed this darkness to an eclipse of the sun.[48] This reveals that about twenty years after the death of Christ, non-believers were still trying to give explanations for the miraculous events of Christ's life.

In 115 AD, a Roman historian named Cornelius Tacitus wrote about the great fire of Rome which occurred during Nero's reign. Tacitus reported that Nero blamed the fire on a group of people called Christians, and he tortured them for it. Tacitus stated that the Christians had been named after their founder "Christus." Tacitus said that Christus had been executed by Pontius Pilate during the reign of Tiberius (14-37 AD). Tacitus related that the "superstition" of the Christians had been stopped for a short time, but then once again broke out, spreading from Judaea all the way to Rome. He said that multitudes of Christians (based on their own confessions to be followers of Christ) were thrown to wild dogs, crucified, or burned to death. Tacitus added

---

[48]Habermas, *Ancient Evidence*, 93.

that their persecutions were not really for the good of the public; their deaths merely satisfied the cruelty of Nero himself.[49]

These statements by Tacitus are consistent with the New Testament records. Even Tacitus' report of the stopping of the "superstition" and then its breaking out again appears to be his attempt to explain how the death of Christ stifled the spreading of the gospel, but then the Christian message was once again preached, this time spreading more rapidly. This is perfectly consistent with the New Testament record. The New Testament reports that Christ's disciples went into hiding during His arrest and death. After Jesus rose from the dead (three days after the crucifixion), He filled His disciples with the Holy Spirit (about fifty days after the crucifixion), and they fearlessly proclaimed the gospel throughout the Roman Empire (Acts 1 and 2).

Both the Bible (Acts 5:33-39) and the Jewish historian Josephus tell their readers that many men claimed to be the Jewish Messiah in ancient times. Eventually, these would-be-messiahs were crushed by the Roman military. Once the self-proclaimed Messiah died, his movement died with him. Tacitus tells us that Jesus died and that His movement was stifled temporarily, but then His movement was somehow "jump-started" and spread throughout the Roman Empire. Since dead Messiah equals dead Messiah movement, historians have had a hard time explaining what Tacitus reported: Jesus' Messiah movement died when He died, but then shortly thereafter His movement came back to life. Since the Messiah was supposed to rescue Israel from her enemies (what Jesus will do when He returns), when a supposed Messiah dies without delivering Israel, His movement dies as well. When Jesus died, His Messiah movement died with Him. But, then His Messiah movement came back to life and continues to spread nearly two-thousand years later. Since dead Messiah equals dead Messiah movement, if Jesus' movement was resurrected, the only explanation is that Jesus the

---

[49]Ibid., 87-88.

20

Messiah came back to life as well. Dead Messiah equals dead Messiah movement; resurrected Messiah movement equals resurrected Messiah. Apart from the resurrection, there is no way that Jesus' Messiah movement would have been revived after Jesus' death as reported by Tacitus.

Suetonius was the chief secretary of Emperor Hadrian who reigned over Rome from 117 to 138 AD. Suetonius refers to the riots that occurred in the Jewish community in Rome in 49 AD due to the instigation of "Chrestus." Chrestus is apparently a variant spelling of Christ. Suetonius refers to these Jews being expelled from the city. Seutonius also reports that following the great fire of Rome, Christians were punished. He refers to their religious beliefs as "new and mischievous."[50]

Pliny the Younger, another ancient secular writer, provides evidence for early Christianity. He was a Roman govenor in Asia Minor. His work dates back to 112 AD. He states that Christians assembled on a set day, sangs hymns to Christ as to "a god," vowed not to partake in wicked deeds, and shared "ordinary" food.[51] This shows that by 112 AD, it was already common knowledge that Christians worshiped Christ, sang hymns to Him, lived moral lives, assembled regularly, and partook of common food (probably a reference to the celebration of the Lord's Supper).

The Roman Emperor Trajan also wrote in 112 AD. He gave guidelines for the persecution of Christians. He stated that if a person denies he is a Christian and proves it by worshiping the Roman gods, he must be pardoned for his repentance.[52]

The Roman Emperor Hadrian reigned from 117 to 138 AD. He wrote that Christians should only be punished if there was clear

---

[50]Ibid., 90.

[51]Ibid., 94.

[52]Ibid., 97.

evidence against them. Mere accusations were not enough to condemn a supposed Christian.[53] The significance of these passages found in the writings of Trajan and Hadrian is that it confirms the fact that early Christians were sincere enough about their beliefs to die for them.

The Talmud is the written form of the oral traditions of the ancient Jewish Rabbis. A Talmud passage dating back to between 70 and 200 AD refers to Jesus as one who "practiced sorcery" and led Israel astray. This passage states that Jesus (spelled Yeshu) was hanged (the common Jewish term for crucifixion) on the night before the Passover feast.[54] This is a very significant passage, for it reveals that even the enemies of Christ admitted there were supernatural aspects of Christ's life by desribing Him as one who "practiced sorcery." This source also confirms that Jesus was crucified around the time of the Passover feast.

Another anti-Christian document was the Toledoth Jesu, which dates back to the fifth century AD, but reflects a much earlier Jewish tradition. In this document, the Jewish leaders are said to have paraded the rotting corpse of Christ through the streets of Jerusalem.[55] This obviously did not occur. The earliest preaching of the gospel took place in Jerusalem. Therefore, parading the rotting corpse of Christ through the streets of Jerusalem would have crushed the Christian faith in its embryonic stage. However, some of the other non-Christian authors mentioned above stated that Christianity spread rapidly during the first few decades after Christ's death. The preaching of Christ's resurrection would not have been persuasive if His rotting corpse had been publicly displayed.

It is also interesting to note that the Jewish religious leaders waited quite a long before putting a refutation of the resurrection into print. Certainly, it would have served their best interests to disprove Christ's

---

[53]Ibid.

[54]Ibid., 98.

[55]Ibid., 99-100.

resurrection. But as far as written documents are concerned, the first century Jewish authorities were silent regarding the resurrection of Jesus.

Lucian was a Greek satirist of the second century. He wrote that Christians worshiped a wise man who had been crucified, lived by His laws, and believed themselves to be immortal.[56] Thus, this ancient secular source confirms the New Testament message by reporting the fact that Jesus was worshiped by His earliest followers.

Probably the most interesting of all ancient non-Christian references to the life of Christ is found in the writings of the Jewish historian named Josephus. Josephus was born in 37 or 38 AD and died in 97 AD. At nineteen, he became a Pharisee—a Jewish religious leader and teacher of the Old Testament.[57] The following passage is found in his writings:

> Now there was about this time Jesus, a wise man, if it be lawful to call him a man; for he was a doer of wonderful works, a teacher of such men as receive the truth with pleasure. He drew over to him both many of the Jews and many of the Gentiles. He was (the) Christ. And when Pilate, at the suggestion of the principal men amongst us, had condemned him to the cross, those that loved him at the first did not forsake him; for he appeared to them alive again the third day; as the divine prophets had foretold these and ten thousand other wonderful things concerning him. And the tribe of Christians, so named after him, are not extinct at this day.[58]

Since Josephus was a Jew and not a Christian, many scholars deny that this passage was originally written by him. These scholars believe this text was corrupted by Christians. Gary Habermas, chairman of the the

---

[56]Ibid., 100.

[57]Ibid., 90.

[58]Flavius Josephus, *The Works of Josephus*. Translated by William Whiston. (Peabody: Hendrickson Publishers, 1987), 480.

philosophy department at Liberty University, dealt with this problem in the following manner:

> There are good indications that the majority of the text is genuine. There is no textual evidence against it, and, conversely, there is very good manuscript evidence for this statement about Jesus, thus making it difficult to ignore. Additionally, leading scholars on the works of Josephus have testified that this portion is written in the style of this Jewish historian. Thus we conclude that there are good reasons for accepting this version of Josephus' statement about Jesus, with modifications of questionable words. In fact, it is possible that these modifications can even be accurately ascertained. In 1972 Professor Schlomo Pines of the Hebrew University in Jerusalem released the results of a study on an Arabic manuscript containing Josephus' statement about Jesus. It includes a different and briefer rendering of the entire passage, including changes in the key words listed above. . . (*Ancient Evidence* 91).[59]

Habermas goes on to relate the Arabic version of this debated passage. In this version, Jesus is described as being a wise and virtuous man who had many followers from different nations. He was crucified under Pontius Pilate, but his disciples reported that, three days later, He appeared to them alive. Josephus added that Jesus may have been the Messiah whom the prophets had predicted would come.[60]

It is highly unlikely that both readings of this controversial passage are corrupt. One of these two readings probably represents the original text. The other reading would then be a copy that was tampered with by either a Christian or a non-Christian. Whatever the case may be, even the skeptic should have no problem accepting the Arabic reading. Still, even if only this reading is accepted, it is enough. For it is a first-century testimony from a non-Christian historian that declares that those who

---

[59]Habermas, *Ancient Evidence*, 91.

[60]Ibid., 91-92.

knew Jesus personally claimed that He had appeared to them alive three days after His death by crucifixion under Pilate.

Several things can be learned from this brief survey of ancient non-Christian writings concerning the life of Christ. First, His earliest followers worshiped Him as God. The doctrine of Christ's deity is therefore not a legend or myth developed many years after Christ's death (as was the case with Buddha). Second, they claimed to have seen Him alive three days after His death. Third, Christ's earliest followers faced persecution and martyrdom for their refusal to deny His deity and resurrection. Therefore, the deity and resurrection of Christ were not legends added to the text centuries after its original composition. Instead, these teachings were the focus of the teaching of Christ's earliest followers. They claimed to be eyewitnesses of Christ's miraculous life and were willing to die horrible deaths for their testimonies. Therefore, they were reliable witnesses of who the true Jesus of history was and what He taught.

The Evidence From Ancient Sermons

Christian philosopher J. P. Moreland, in his book *Scaling the Secular City*, discusses another important evidence that indicates the New Testament we have today is an accurate representation of the teachings of the early church leaders—the apostles.[61] Moreland points to the "evangelistic speeches" found in Acts chapters one through twelve as strong evidence that the apostles did proclaim Jesus to be the Jewish Messiah who had died on the cross and rose from the dead, and that these speeches date back to the earliest years of Christianity—the early 30's AD.

Moreland gives five aspects of these speeches indicating they are extremely early. First, these speeches "translate well into Aramaic."

---

[61]J. P. Moreland, *Scaling the Secular City* (Grand Rapids: Baker Book House, 1987), 155-156.

This cannot be said of the sermons found in Acts chapter thirteen and beyond. This probably indicates that these speeches were originally spoken in Aramaic to Jewish audiences.[62] Aramaic was the common language of first-century Judean Jews. Before the gospel was proclaimed to the Gentiles, it was almost exclusively preached to the Jews.

Second, the speeches of Acts chapters one through twelve have a "unique vocabulary, tone, style, and theology" in contrast to the rest of Acts.[63] This shows that in Acts chapters one through twelve we find material that predates the writing of the book of Acts, and that the author of Acts referred to this earlier material to compile Acts one through twelve.

Third, Moreland states that "the theology of these speeches is primitive; that is, it does not reflect a great deal of developed thinking." In other words, these speeches were given before the early church had sufficient time to contemplate the person and works of Jesus to formulate systematic doctrines. Moreland shows that the Messiahship of Jesus is emphasized, rather than His deity (which is what we would expect to be the case when the gospel was first preached to Jewish audiences). Primitive phrases are used to refer to Jesus such as "Jesus the Nazarene" and "thy holy Child Jesus." These phrases were not commonly used by the early church after the first decade of its existence. Moreland adds that a primitive concept of redemption is used in these speeches—Jesus is viewed as the one who redeems the nation of Israel, rather than as the Savior of the world.[64]

Fourth, the vocabulary, style, and emphasis of the speeches given by Peter in the first twelve chapters of Acts are very similar to the material found in 1 Peter and the Gospel of Mark (the early church

---

[62]Ibid., 155.

[63]Ibid.

[64]Ibid.

fathers told us that Mark received his Gospel from the Apostle Peter). This gives one the impression that the speeches were in fact given by the same person—the Apostle Peter.[65]

And, fifth, according to the first two chapters of Acts, these speeches represent the earliest preaching of the gospel and were preached in Jerusalem just seven weeks after Jesus was crucified. Moreland reasons that this information (the preaching in Jerusalem and the seven week gap) is probably reliable since it would have been counter-productive for the early church to invent the seven week interval before the gospel was publicly proclaimed.[66] Why have the apostles wait seven weeks before proclaiming Christ's resurrection unless that is what actually happened? But that means that the early church actually preached that Jesus had risen from the dead just seven weeks after He was crucified. The resurrection was not a legend that evolved into existence over a prolonged period of time; it was publicly preached in Jerusalem (the easiest place on earth to refute a resurrection hoax) only weeks after Christ's death.

Moreland concludes that the evidence indicates these sermons are extremely early, taking us back to within weeks of Christ's death. Yet, when we examine the content of these speeches, we see that Jesus is proclaimed as the Jewish Messiah and the Savior, and that the apostles declare themselves to be eyewitnesses of His resurrection (Acts 2:22-24, 32, 38; 3:15; 4:10-12; 5:30-32; 10:38-43).[67] Therefore, the supernatural aspects of Jesus' life were proclaimed by the early church from the beginning; the miraculous aspects of Christ's life are not legends, but the testimony of the people who knew Him.

---

[65]Ibid., 156.

[66]Ibid.

[67]Ibid.

The Evidence From Ancient Creeds

The writings of both the apostolic fathers and ancient non-Christian authors declare that the earliest Christians did in fact teach that Jesus is God and that He rose from the dead. We have seen that the manuscript evidence for the New Testament is stronger than that of any other ancient writing. Ancient sermons found in the first twelve chapters of Acts also show the New Testament portrait of Jesus to be accurate. Another piece of evidence for the authenticity and reliability of the New Testament manuscripts is the ancient creeds found in the New Testament itself.

Most scholars, whether liberal or conservative, date Paul's epistles before the Gospels were put into written form.[68] Just as the teachings of the Jewish Rabbis had originally been passed on orally, it appears that the Gospel was first spread in the form of oral creeds and hymns.[69] J. P. Moreland states that Paul's epistles contain many of these pre-Pauline creeds and hymns, that they were originally spoken in the Aramaic tongue (the Hebrew language of Christ's day), and that most scholars date these creeds and hymns between 33 AD and 48 AD.[70] Since Paul's writings are dated in the 50's or 60's AD by most scholars, the creeds he recorded in his letters point to an oral tradition which predates his writings. Most scholars will at least admit that these ancient creeds originated before 50 AD.[71]

Excerpts from some of these ancient creeds found in the letters of Paul are as follows:

---

[68]McDowell and Wilson, 168-170.

[69]Ibid., 170.

[70]Moreland, Scaling, 148-149.

[71]Ibid.

. . . that if you confess with your mouth Jesus as Lord, and believe in your heart that God raised Him from the dead, you shall be saved (Rom. 10:9).

Have this attitude in yourselves which was also in Christ Jesus, who, although He existed in the form of God, did not regard equality with God a thing to be grasped, but emptied Himself, taking the form of a bondservant, and being made in the likeness of men. And being found in appearance as a man, He humbled Himself by becoming obedient to the point of death, even death on a cross. Therefore also God highly exalted Him, and bestowed on Him the name which is above every name, that at the name of Jesus every knee should bow, of those who are in heaven, and on earth, and under the earth, and that every tongue should confess that Jesus Christ is Lord, to the glory of God the Father (Phil. 2:5-11).

And He [Christ] is the image of the invisible God, the first-born of all creation. For by Him all things were created, both in the heavens and on earth, visible and invisible, whether thrones or dominions or rulers or authorities—all things have been created by Him and for Him. And He is before all things, and in Him all things hold together (Col. 1:15-17).

The creed found in 1 Corinthians 15:3-8 provides extremely strong and early evidence for Christ's resurrection. It is often assumed by anti-Christian skeptics that the resurrection of Jesus Christ from the dead is nothing more than an ancient myth or legend, having no basis in historical fact. However, this is not the case. In the Apostle Paul's First Letter to the Corinthians, we find excellent eyewitness testimony concerning the resurrection that nearly dates back to the event itself. The Apostle Paul wrote:

For I delivered to you as of first importance what I also received, that Christ died for our sins according to the Scriptures, and that He was buried, and that He was raised on the third day according to the

Scriptures, and that He appeared to Cephas, then to the twelve. After that He appeared to more than five hundred brethren at one time, most of whom remain until now, but some have fallen asleep; then He appeared to James, then to all the apostles; and last of all, as it were to one untimely born, He appeared to me also (1 Cor. 15:3-8).

Most New Testament scholars, liberal and conservative alike, agree that this passage is an ancient creed or hymn formulated by the early church. In our task of ascertaining when the creed of 1 Corinthians 15 was created, it is first necessary to determine when Paul wrote 1 Corinthians. In this way, we will establish the latest possible date for the creed. We can then work our way back in time from that date, following any clues based upon the internal evidence found in the creed itself. Christian philosopher J. P. Moreland has correctly stated that for the past one hundred years almost all New Testament critics have accepted the Pauline authorship of First Corinthians.[72] A comparison of First Corinthians 16 with Acts 18, 19, and 20 provides strong evidence that First Corinthians was written by Paul in 55 AD while in Ephesus. Scholars such as John A. T. Robinson, Henry C. Thiessen, A. T. Robertson, Douglas Moo, Leon Morris, and D. A. Carson all concur that 1 Corinthians was written in the mid 50's AD.[73]

We have established 55 AD as the date for the composition of First Corinthians. This means that the ancient creed quoted by Paul in First Corinthians 15:3-8 had to originate before this date. However, there is strong evidence found in the creed itself that points to its development at a much earlier time.

Christian apologist Gary Habermas discusses at least eight pieces of evidence from within the creed that indicate a very early date. First, the

---

[72]Moreland, *Scaling*, 148.

[73]Leon Morris, *1 Corinthians*. (Leicester, England: Intervarsity Press, 1995), 30-31.

terms "delivered" and "received" have been shown to be technical rabbinic terms used for the passing on of sacred tradition.[74] Second, Paul admitted that this statement was not his own creation and that he had received it from others. Third, scholars agree that some of the words in the creed are non-Pauline terms and are clearly Jewish. These phrases include "for our sins," "according to the Scriptures," "He has been raised," "the third day," "He was seen," and "the twelve." Fourth, the creed is organized into a stylized and parallel form; it appears to have been an oral creed or hymn in the early church.[75] Fifth, the creed shows evidence of being of a Semitic origin and, thus, points to a source that predates Paul's translation of it into Greek. This can be seen in the use of "Cephas" for Peter, for "Cephas" is Aramaic for Peter (which is Petros in the Greek). J. P. Moreland notes additional evidence for the Semitic origin of this creed by relating that the poetic style of the early creed is Hebraic.[76] Sixth, Habermas reasons that Paul probably received this creed around 36-38 AD, just three years after his conversion, when he met with Peter and James in Jerusalem, as recorded by Paul in Galatians 1:18-19.[77] Jesus' death occurred around 30 to 33 AD, and Paul was converted between 31 and 35 AD. Seventh, Habermas states that, due to the above information, "numerous critical theologians" date the creed "from three to eight years after Jesus' crucifixion." Eighth, since it would have taken a period of time for the beliefs to become formalized into a creed or hymn, the beliefs behind the creed must date back to the event itself.[78]

Hence, there is strong evidence that the creed of First Corinthians 15:3-8 originated between three to eight years after Christ's crucifixion,

---

[74]Habermas, *Ancient Evidence*, 124.

[75]Ibid., 125.
[76]Moreland, *Scaling*, 150.

[77]Habermas, *Ancient Evidence*, 125.

[78]Ibid.

and that the beliefs which underlie this creed must therefore go back to the event itself. Now we must briefly examine the content of this ancient creed.

First, the creed mentions the death and burial of Christ. Second, it states that Christ was raised on the third day. Third, it lists several post-resurrection appearances of Christ. These include appearances to Peter, to the twelve apostles, to over 500 persons at one time, to James (the Lord's brother), to all the apostles, and, finally an appearance to Paul himself.

It should be noted that scholars differ as to the exact contents of this ancient creed in its most primitive form. It seems that Paul added verse eight (detailing his own eyewitness account) to the original creed, as well as a portion of verse six (a reminder that most of the 500 witnesses were still alive). This in no way lessons the force of this ancient creed. In fact, it strengthens it as evidence for the resurrection, for Paul adds his own testimony and encourages his readers to question the many eyewitnesses still living in his day. Whatever the case, most New Testament scholars accept a large enough portion of the creed for it to be considered a valuable piece of eyewitness evidence for the resurrection of Christ from the dead.

Having argued for a very early date for its origin, we must now ascertain the evidential value of this creed. Simply stated, the early date of the First Corinthians 15 creed proves that the resurrection accounts found in the New Testament are not legends. Christian philosopher William Lane Craig, while commenting on the work of the great Roman historian A. N. Sherwin-White, stated that "even two generations is too short a time span to allow legendary tendencies to wipe out the hard core of historical facts."[79] If two generations is not enough time for legends to develop, then there is no way that a resurrection legend could emerge in only three to eight years.

---

[79]William Lane Craig, *Reasonable Faith* (Wheaton: Crossway Books, 1994), 285.

It should also be noted that, in this creed, Paul is placing his apostolic credentials on the line by encouraging his Corinthian critics to check out his account with the eyewitnesses who were still alive. These eyewitnesses not only included over 500 people, but also Peter, James, and the other apostles—the recognized leaders of the early church (Gal. 2:9). It is highly improbable that Paul would fabricate the creed and jeopardize his own position in the early church.

Finally, it should be obvious to any open-minded person who examines the evidence that Paul was a man of integrity. He was not lying. Not only did he put his reputation and position in the early church on the line, but he was also willing to suffer and die for Christ. Men do not die for what they know to be a hoax. Paul was a reliable and sincere witness to the resurrection of Christ.

The creed of First Corinthians 15:3-8 provides us with reliable eyewitness testimony for the bodily resurrection of Jesus Christ. Not only did Paul testify that he had seen the risen Christ, but he also identified many other witnesses to the resurrection that could have been interrogated. Contrary to the futile speculations of liberal scholars, Paul was not devising myths behind closed doors. No, from the beginning he was preaching a risen Savior who had conquered death and the grave, a risen Savior who had met him on the road to Damascus and changed his life forever.

When taken together, these ancient creeds (Rom. 10:9; Phil. 2:5-11; Col. 1:15-17; 1 Cor. 15:3-8; etc.) clearly prove that the first generation Christians believed that Jesus had bodily risen from the dead, that He is God, and that salvation comes through Him.[80] The followers of Buddha attributed deity to the founder of their religion centuires after his death.[81] However, the earliest followers of Christ, those who knew Jesus

---

[80]Moreland, *Scaling*, 149.

[81]Josh McDowell and Don Stewart. *Handbook of Today's Religions* (San Bernardino: Here's Life Publishers, 1983), 307-308.

personally, considered Him to be God during their lifetimes.[82] It is almost universally recognised by New Testament scholars today that these creeds were formulated before 50 AD, some of these creeds going back to the early 30s AD. Therefore, these creeds represent the gospel in its original form, the gospel preached by the early church—the apostles themselves.

Hence, the belief in Christ's deity and resurrection is not based on later corruptions of the New Testament text as liberal scholars believe. The doctrines of Christ's deity and resurrection are not legends that took centuries to develop. These doctrines were held by the first generation church, those who knew Jesus personally. The gospel message found in the New Testament is the same message proclaimed by the apostles themselves.

Less than twenty years after Christ's death, hymns were already being sung in Christian churches attributing deity to Christ. The apostles were still alive and had the authority to supress the doctrine of Christ's deity if it was a heresy; but, they did not. All the available evidence indicates that they not only condoned it, but that it was their own teaching. Therefore, liberal scholars such as John Hick have no justification for their claims that the deity of Christ was a legend that developed near the end of the first century AD.[83] The historical evidence indicates that the Christian church always believed in Christ's deity. Therefore, to deny that Christ claimed to be God is to call the apostles liars.

Nearly 2,000 years after the death of Christ a forum of liberal scholars called the "Jesus Seminar" began meeting in 1985. These scholars voted to decide which biblical passages they believed Jesus

---

[82]Moreland, *Scaling*, 150.

[83]John Hick, *The Center of Christianity* (New York: Harper and Row, 1978), 27-29.

actually said.[84] This is ironic since the evidence shows that Christianity proclaimed Christ's deity and resurrection from its inception. The early church accepted the deity of Christ and His bodily resurrection. The first believers were willing to suffer horrible persecution for these beliefs. Sincere eyewitness testimony should not be ignored by contemporary scholars.

The Letters of Paul and the Historical Jesus

Liberal scholars, as well as many evangelical scholars who accept liberal presuppositions, believe that Paul's letters comprise the earliest New Testament writings. Several of Paul's letters (i.e., Rom., 1 Cor., 2 Cor., Gal., Phil., 1 Thess., and Philem.) are accepted as authentic by the vast majority of New Testament critics today. The reasons given by liberal scholars for rejecting the other six Pauline letters (i.e., Eph., Col., 2 Thess., 1 Tim., 2 Tim., and Titus) are not convincing. The early church fathers accepted all thirteen of Paul's letters as being authentically written by him. The burden of proof is on the liberal scholars if they wish to deny Pauline authorship of these other letters. These letters were collected very early by the church, and there is no reason to assume that the early church was mistaken. The apostolic fathers (i.e., leaders in the early church who were trained by the apostles themselves) quoted from or alluded to all thirteen of Paul's letters as authoritative by 110 AD.[85] Are we really to believe that the early church leaders were mistaken? Again, the burden of proof is on those who choose to deny the Pauline authorship of these letters.

In Paul's letters (both the accepted letters and the debated letters), one can find an outline of the life, ministry, and teachings of Jesus. Paul

---

[84]J. P. Moreland and Michael J. Wilkins, *Jesus Under Fire* (Grand Rapids: Zondervan Publishing House, 1995), 2-3.

[85]Barnett, *New Testament*, 39-42.

Barnett lists aspects of Jesus' life known and proclaimed by Paul.[86] Paul related that Jesus was a descendent of both Abraham and David (Gal. 3:16; Rom. 1:3), that He was born of a woman under the Jewish Law (Gal. 4:4), and that He lived a life of humble service despite the fact that He was rejected and insulted during His life (Phil. 2:5-8; Rom. 15:3). Paul knew that James was Jesus' brother and that Jesus had other brothers (Gal. 1:19; 1 Cor. 9:5). Paul knew the Apostle Peter enough to know that Peter was married (1 Cor. 9:5). Paul knew of the Last Supper, the betrayal of Christ, and His trial before Pilate (1 Cor. 11:23-26; 1 Tim. 6:13). Paul also taught that Jesus is God (Phil. 2:6; Rom. 10:9; Titus 2:13; Col. 2:9), He is Messiah (Gal. 1:1; Rom. 1:1), He is Savior (Titus 2:13), and He died on the cross for our sins (1 Cor. 15:3). Paul relates that Judean Jews played a role in Jesus' death (1 Thess. 2:14-15), and that Jesus was buried, but rose from the dead and appeared to numerous people on several occassions (1 Cor. 15:4-8).

It must be remembered that Paul recorded these events of Christ's life just twenty to thirty years after Christ's death. Still, Larry Hurtado of the University of Edinburgh points out that the evidence for the historical Jesus found in Paul's writings is stronger than that. Hurtado relates that Paul constantly argued for his views when others in the church disagreed with him. Yet, states Hurtado, Paul never argues that Jesus is God or Messiah, or that Jesus rose from the dead. He merely states these doctrines as if they were universally accepted by the Christian church at the time of his writings. Hence, Hurtado argues that the worship of Jesus as God, the acknowledgment of Him as Messiah, and the belief in His resurrection all date back to the early 30s AD—the approximate time Paul met with the leaders of the Jerusalem church.[87]

---

[86]Ibid., 140-141.

[87]Larry W. Hurtado, *Lord Jesus Christ: Devotion to Jesus in Earliest Christianity* (Grand Rapids: William B. Eerdmans Publishing, 2003), 101, 128-129, 131-137, 650.

Paul was not an innovator; he did not create a new religion; he taught the same Gospel as Peter and John—the original followers of Jesus.

Jesus was crucified around 30 to 33 AD.[88] Paul became a Christian just a year or two later (31-35 AD?). Just three years after he was converted, about 34 to 37 AD, Paul traveled to Jerusalem to meet with the leaders of the Jerusalem church.[89] At that time, Paul met with Peter and James, the half-brother of Jesus (Gal. 1:18-19). Fourteen years after his conversion (45-48 AD?), Paul again went to Jerusalem, and he and Barnabas met with Peter, James, and John.[90] These leaders of the Jerusalem church acknowledged that Paul and Barnabas were preaching the same Gospel as they were; they extended the right hand of fellowship to Paul and Barnabas (Gal. 2:1-10). This would not have occurred if Paul was preaching a different Gospel. In short, Paul's Gospel of Jesus as the Messiah, God, and risen Savior was the same Gospel as the original followers of Jesus proclaimed.

Liberal New Testament critics are guilty of trying to invent a "Jesus of the gaps." These critics believe that Paul wrote the earliest portions of the New Testament, yet they reject the Jesus whom Paul proclaims. Therefore, they contend that the true Jesus of history was transformed into imaginary Jesus of Paul's writings. However, this cannot be the case. Even these critics do not question Paul's honesty; yet, Paul claimed that the leaders of the Jerusalem church confirmed that his Gospel was one and the same as their's. In other words, there is no gap. Paul's writings, the ancient sermons of Acts chapters one through twelve, and the ancient creeds found in the New Testament all take us back to Christianity's earliest years, and, at this early date, we find the same Jesus found in Paul's letters and the rest of the New Testament as

---

[88]Ben Witherington III, *The Paul Quest: The Renewed Search for the Jew of Tarsus* (Downers Grove, Illinois: InterVarsity Press, 1998), 307.

[89]Ibid., 309.

[90]Ibid., 317.

well. In short, there can be no "Jesus of the gaps" because there are no gaps (see 1 Cor. 15:1-11). We can trace the Gospel to the early 30s AD, and, when we do, we find that the true Jesus of history is identical to the Jesus found in the New Testament.

The First-Century AD Dates of the New Testament Books

Liberal critics acknowledge most of Paul's writings as having been authored by the Apostle Paul between 50 AD and 64-65 AD. But, arguments for early dates of other New Testament books are also very convincing. We will look at three New Testament books to illustrate this point.

Both the Gospel of Luke and the Book of Acts were written to the same recipient—a man named Theophilus (Luke 1:1-4; Acts 1:1-3). The prologues of these books show us that Acts is the sequel of Luke; therefore, Luke was written before Acts. Acts focuses on the key characters Peter, Paul, and James (the half-brother of Jesus), yet it does not record their deaths. Peter and Paul died between 64 and 67 AD, while James died in 62 AD. Since Acts records the deaths of people less significant to the purposes of the book (i.e., Ananias, Sapphira, Stephen, James son of Zebedee, and Herod Agrippa), it appears that Acts must have been written before Peter, Paul, and James were executed (before 62 AD). Also, though Jerusalem is one of the major cities of the Book of Acts and the temple plays a key role in Acts, no mention is made of the war with the Romans (started 66 AD) and the destruction of the temple (70 AD). This is further confirmation that Acts was written early. Acts is a book filled with adventure, yet it ends anti-climatically with Paul in Rome in chains in 61 AD. This makes no sense unless Acts was completed in 61 AD and then sent to Theophilus. And, since Acts is the sequel to Luke's Gospel, the Gospel of Luke had to be written at an even earlier date. This is also confirmed by the fact that Paul quotes from Luke's Gospel as Scripture (1 Tim. 5:18). Therefore, both Luke and Acts were written before 62 AD.

The Book of Hebrews was written for the purpose of trying to prevent Jews who had accepted Jesus from abandoning the Christian faith due to persecution. The author of the Book of Hebrews argues that the temple priests are still standing and still offering sacrifices. Therefore, their animal sacrifices have failed to take away our sins. The author of Hebrews then reasons that since Jesus is seated at the Father's right hand, His work is done and His sacrifice of Himself on the cross has accomplished its purpose—our sins are forgiven. This argument makes no sense if the Book of Hebrews was written after 70 AD (the year the temple was destroyed by the Romans). If Hebrews was written after 70 AD, the author would have argued that it is impossible for his readers to return to the animal sacrifices since God allowed the temple to be destroyed. Instead, his argument only works if the temple is still standing and the temple sacrifices are still being offered. Hence, Hebrews was written before 70 AD.

Paul's accepted writings, Luke, Acts, and Hebrews all portray Jesus as God, Messiah, and risen Savior. Yet, these books were all written at least between 50 and 70 AD. The ancient creeds and sermons, dating to the early 30s AD, found in the New Testament, also paint the same picture of Jesus. Hence, the Jesus of the New Testament can be traced all the way back to the start of the church. The biblical Jesus is not a legend; Paul was not an innovator. The Jesus of the Bible is the true Jesus of history.

As the chart below indicates, there exists an unbroken chain of evidence for Jesus' claims to be God, Messiah, and the risen Savior who died for our sins. There is no gap—there is absolutely no room for legends or perversions of the Gospel message to take place.

Dates	Evidences
30's & 40's AD	ancient creeds found in New Testament ancient sermons (Acts 1-12)

	hypothetical "Q" document the Book of James Matthew, Mark, Luke ? (Could they be this early?) Paul's teachings before he wrote his letters
50's & 60's AD	Paul's writings Gospels (if we accept conservative dates) Gospel of John (could it be written this early?) Acts & Luke (written before 61 AD) Hebrews (written before 70 AD) Possible NT fragments (Dead Sea Scrolls) The Didache (teaching of the 12 Apostles)
70's-90's AD	Gospels (if we accept liberal dates) Non-Pauline New Testament letters? Clement of Rome's letter Epistle of Barnabas Shepherd of Hermas
90's-150's AD	Writings of other apostolic fathers Writings of ancient secular authors Fragment of John 18
150's -325 AD	Extant New Testament manuscripts Early church fathers before Nicea

325 AD-today	Early church after Nicea to the reformers to the conservative evangelical church today

The Opinions of the Experts

The testimonies of some of the world's leading experts can be called upon to further verify the authenticity and reliability of the New Testament manuscripts. Dr. John A. T. Robinson, one of England's leading New Testament critics, came to the conclusion that the entire New Testament was written before the fall of Jerusalem in 70 AD.[91]

Sir William Ramsey was one of the world's greatest archaeologists. His thorough investigation into Luke's Book of Acts led him to the conclusion that Acts was a mid-first century document that was historically reliable.[92] William F. Albright is one of the world's foremost biblical archaeologists. He stated that there is no evidential basis for dating any New Testament book after 80 AD.[93] Sir Frederic Kenyon was one of the world's leading experts on ancient manuscripts. His research led him to conclude that the New Testament is essentially the same as when it was originally written.[94]

Millar Burrows, the great archaeologist from Yale, stated that there is no doubt that archaeological research has strengthened confidence in the historical reliability of the Bible. Burrows also stated that the

---

[91]McDowell, *Evidence*, 63.

[92]Roy Abraham Varghese, *The Intellectuals Speak Out About God* (Dallas: Lewis and Stanley Publishers, 1984), 267-268.

[93]Ibid., 267.

[94]Ibid., 274.

skepticism of liberal scholars is based on their prejudice against the supernatural, rather than on the evidence itself.[95]

F. F. Bruce, New Testament scholar from Manchester University in England, stated that if the New Testament writings had been secular works, no scholar would question their authenticity. Bruce believes that the evidence for the New Testament outweighs the evidence for many classical works which have never been doubted.[96]

Bruce Metzger was a famous textual critic from Princeton. He has stated that the New Testament has more evidence in its favor than any other writings from ancient Greek or Latin literature.[97]

It is clear that the evidence favors the authenticity and reliability of the New Testament. Scholars who do not allow their bias against the supernatural to influence their conclusions have recognized this fact. Scholars who reject the reliability of the New Testament manuscripts do so because they chose to go against the overwhelming evidence. However, such a rejection is not true scholarship; it is an a priori assumption. If one uses neutral presuppositions rather than liberal, anti-supernatural presuppositions, then the outcome is clear: the New Testament portrait of Jesus is historically accurate.

Jesus' Inner Circle

One more point in favor of New Testament reliability needs to be mentioned. It is interesting to note that a strong case can be made from the writngs of the early church fathers that all the books found in the New Testament can be traced back to the authority of Jesus' inner circle—those who knew Jesus more intimately than anyone else. The early church (i.e., Papias, Ireneaus, Clement of Alexandria, Tertullian,

---

[95]McDowell, Evidence, 66.

[96]Varghese, 274.

[97]Ibid., 205.

etc.) told us that Matthew wrote the Gospel bearing his name. Since Matthew was one of the original apostles, he was in Jesus' inner circle. The early church also told us that John the apostle wrote his Gospel, his three epistles, and the Book of Revelation. Peter, another apostle, wrote two epistles and his preaching formed the basis for Mark's Gospel. The apostle Paul wrote thirteen epistles. Luke was Paul's colleague and he wrote his Gospel and the Book of Acts. The author of Hebrews knew Timothy (a colleague of Paul) and apparently knew Paul's theology; hence, he was probably also an associate of the apsotle Paul. And, finally, James and Jude were Jesus' half brothers, and they each authored a New Testament epistle. Hence, all twenty-seven New Testament books can be traced back to Matthew, John, Peter, Paul, or Jesus' brothers (i.e., Jesus' inner circle). This explains why these twenty-seven books were canonized (i.e., accepted as the list of books that belong in the Bible), whereas many other books were rejected.

Conclusion

Evidence from the existing New Testament manuscripts, from the writings of the apostolic fathers, from the works of ancient secular authors, from the ancient sermons, creeds, and hymns found in the New Testament, and from the opinions of the world's leading experts has been examined. Evidence from Paul's writings, Luke, Acts, and Hebrews has been presented. All this evidence leads to the conclusion that the existing New Testament manuscripts are reliable and authentic testimony of what the apostles wrote. The Jesus of the New Testament is the Jesus of history. A person is free to deny this conclusion, but to do so is to go against all the available evidence. The key point is that the original apostles taught that Jesus rose from the dead, and that He claimed to be God incarnate and the Savior of the world.

Suggested Reading

Barnett, Paul. *Is the New Testament Reliable?* Downers Grove: InterVarsity Press, 2003.

Barnett, Paul *Messiah: Jesus—the Evidence of History*. Nottingham: Inter Varsity Press, 2009.

Bauckham, Richard. *The Testimony of the Beloved Disciple*. Grand Rapids: Baker Book House, 2007.

Bauckham, Richard. *Jesus and the Eyewitnesses*. Grand Rapids: Eerdmans, 2006.

Blomberg, Craig. *The Historical Reliability of the Gospels*. Downers Grove: Inter-Varsity Press,   1987.

Bock, Darrell and Daniel Wallace. *Dethroning Jesus: Exposing Popular Culture's Quest to Unseat the Biblical Christ*. Nashville: Thomas Nelson Publishers, 2007).

Boyd, Gregory A. *Cynic Sage or Son of God?* Wheaton: Victor Books, 1995.

Boyd, Gregory A. and Paul Rhodes Eddy. *The Jesus Legend—A Case for the Historical Reliability of the Synoptic Tradition*. Grand Rapids: Baker Book House, 2007.

Brown, Raymond E. *An Introduction to New Testament Christology*. New York: Paulist Press, 1994.

Bruce, F. F. *The Canon of Scripture*. Downers Grove: InterVarsity Press, 1988.

Bruce, F. F. *The New Testament Documents: Are They Reliable?* Downers Grove: InterVarsity Press, 1960.

Carson, D. A., Douglas J. Moo, and Leon Morris. *An Introduction to the New Testament*. Grand Rapids: Zondervan Publishing House, 1992.

Copan, Paul, ed., *Will the Real Jesus Please Stand Up? A Debate Between William Lane Craig and John Dominic Crossan*. Grand Rapids: Baker Book House, 1998.

Craig, William Lane. *Reasonable Faith*. Wheaton: Crossway Books, 1994.

Craig, William Lane. *The Son Rises*. Eugene: Wipf and Stock Publishers, 1981.

Erickson, Millard J. *The Word Became Flesh*. Grand Rapids: Baker Book House, 1991.

Evans, Craig A. *Fabricating Jesus*. Downers Grove: InterVarsity Press, 2006.

Geisler, Norman L. *Christian Apologetics*. Grand Rapids: Baker Book House, 1976.

Geisler, Norman L. *Miracles and the Modern Mind*. Grand Rapids: Baker Book House, 1992.

Geisler, Norman L. and William E. Nix. *A General Introduction to the Bible*. Chicago: Moody Press, 1986.

Geisler, Norman L. and Frank Turek. *I Don't Have Enough Faith to be an Atheist*. Wheaton: Crossway Books, 2004.

Geivett, R. Douglas and Gary R. Habermas. Editors. *In Defense of Miracles*. Downers Grove: Inter Varsity, 1997.

Habermas, Gary R. *Ancient Evidence for the Life of Jesus*. Nashville: Thomas Nelson Publishers, 1984.

Habermas, Gary R. *The Historical Jesus*. Joplin, Missouri: College Press, 1996.

Habermas, Gary R. *The Resurrection of Jesus*. Lanham: University Press of America, 1984.

Habermas, Gary R. *The Risen Jesus and Future Hope*. Lanham: Rowan and Littlefield, 2003.

Habermas, Gary R. and Michael R. Licona. *The Case for the Resurrection of Jesus*. Grand Rapids: Kregel Publications, 2004.

Habermas, Gary R. and Antony G. N. Flew. *Did Jesus Rise From the Dead?* Edited by Terry L. Miethe. New York: Harper and Row, 1987.

Habermas, Gary R. and Antony G. N. Flew. *Resurrected? An Atheist and Theist Dialogue*. Edited by John F. Ankerberg. Lanham: Rowan and Littlefield, 2005.

Hume, David. *An Inquiry Concerning Human Understanding*. New York: The Liberal Arts Press, 1955.

Hurtado, Larry W. *Lord Jesus Christ: Devotion to Jesus in Earliest Christianity*. Grand Rapids: William B. Eerdmans Publishing, 2003.

Josephus, Flavius. *The Works of Josephus*. Translated by William Whiston. Peabody: Hendrickson Publishers, 1987.

Kostenberger, Andreas J. and Michael J. Kruger. *The Heresy of Orthodoxy: How Contemporary Culture's Fascination with Diversity Has Reshaped Our Understanding of Early Christianity*. Wheaton, Illinois: Crossway Books, 2010.

Lewis, C. S. *Miracles*. New York: Collier Books, 1960.

Lightfoot, J. B. and J. R. Harmer. Translators. *The Apostolic Fathers*. Grand Rapids: Baker Book House, 1984.

Marshall, I. Howard. *The Origins of New Testament Christology*. Downers Grove: InterVarsity Press, 1990.

McDowell, Josh. *The New Evidence that Demands a Verdict*. Nashville: Thomas Nelson Publishers, 1999.

McDowell, Josh. *Evidence that Demands a Verdict*. San Bernardino: Here's Life Publishers, 1974.

McDowell, Josh and Bill Wilson. *He Walked Among Us*. San Bernardino: Here's Life Publishers, 1988.

Metzger, Bruce M. *The Canon of the New Testament*. Oxford: Clarendon press, 1987.

Moreland, J. P. *Scaling the Secular City*. Grand Rapids: Baker Book House, 1987.

Morris, Leon. *1 Corinthians*. Leicester, England: Intervarsity Press, 1995.

Nash, Ronald. *The Gospel and the Greeks: Did the New Testament Borrow from Pagan Thought?* Phillipsburg: Presbyterian and Reformed, 1992.

Reymond, Robert L. *Jesus: Divine Messiah*. Phillipsburg: Presbyterian & Reformed Publishing, 1990.

Robinson, John A. T. *Redating the New Testament*. Eugene: Wipf and Stock Publishers, 1976.

Sherwin-White, A. N. *Roman Society and Roman Law in the New Testament*. Oxford: Clarendon, 1963.

Strobel, Lee. *The Case for Christ*. Grand Rapids: Zondervan Publishing House, 1998.

Strobel, Lee. *The Case for the Real Jesus*. Grand Rapids: Zondervan Publishing House, 2007.

Thiede, Carsten P. *The Dead Sea Scrolls and the Jewish Origins of Christianity*. New York: Palgrave, 2000.

Thiede, Carsten P. *Rekindling the Word*. Valley Forge: Trinity Press, 1995.

Thiede, Carsten P. and Matthew D'Ancona. *Eyewitness to Jesus*. New York: Doubleday, 1996.

Thiessen, Henry C. *Introduction to the New Testament.* Grand
Rapids: William B. Eerdmans Publishing Company, 1987.

Thomas, Robert L. and F. David Farnell, eds. *The Jesus Crisis.* Grand
Rapids: Kregel Publications, 1998.

Thomas, Robert L., ed. *Three Views of the Origins of the Synoptic
Gospels.* Grand Rapids: Kregel Publications, 2002.

Varghese, Roy Abraham. *The Intellectuals Speak Out About God.*
Dallas: Lewis and Stanley Publishers, 1984.

Wenham, John. *Redating Matthew, Mark, and Luke.* Downers Grove:
Inter Varsity Press, 1992.

Wilkins, Michael J. and J. P. Moreland. Eds. *Jesus Under Fire.* Grand
Rapids: Zondervan Publishing House, 1995.

Witherington III, Ben. *The Gospel Code.* Downers Grove:
InterVarsity Press, 2004.

Witherington III, Ben. *The Jesus Quest: The Third Search for the Jew
of Nazareth.* Downers Grove, Illinois: InterVarsity Press, 1997.

Wright, N. T. *The Contemporary Quest for Jesus.* Minneapolis:
Fortress Press, 1996.

Wright, N. T. *The Resurrection of the Son of God.* Minneapolis:
Fortress Press, 2003.

Made in the USA
Middletown, DE
23 August 2019